Research

By
TEDDY MEISTER

COPYRIGHT © 2007 Mark Twain Media, Inc.

ISBN 978-1-58037-426-2

Printing No. CD-404075

Mark Twain Media, Inc., Publishers
Distributed by Carson-Dellosa Publishing Company, Inc.

The purchase of this book entitles the buyer to reproduce the student pages for classroom use only. Other permissions may be obtained by writing Mark Twain Media, Inc., Publishers.

All rights reserved. Printed in the United States of America

Table of Contents

Introduction

Knowledge is knowing…and knowing how to find out.

— Alvin Toffler

Research will help students put the *search* in *research*. Each ready-to-go topic will enable students to explore a variety of topics as independent or teacher-directed assignments.

Topics are designed to build and enhance reference skills for a range of reading levels from grades 4 through 8 in a differentiated instructional setting. Though alphabetically listed, they can be used in any order or integrated with the ongoing curriculum.

Each self-contained research sheet is multi-disciplined. They are flexible for use as curriculum enrichment, activities for more able independent learners, classroom centers, unit launchers, small- or large-group activities, or take-home assignments. Topic sheets can be copied, laminated, and stored in a class box for students to self-select topics of their own interest. Encourage students to explore the world of research.

How to Use *Research*

Each *Research* topic sheet is organized in the following way:

READ: A brief summary is presented to provide a topic overview and pique student interest.

RESEARCH: This section contains three to five research-based activities that involve higher cognitive processes. It will allow students to creatively apply information learned in a variety of projects and products. Students can select activities they want to do, or the teacher might require specific activities. Activities can be used for extra credit work. Resources are sometimes listed with the activities. It would be helpful to first check the availability of general reference materials, dictionaries, computers, almanacs, and other sources that are available in the library or school media center. If there are other libraries in the area, they could serve as alternative places for students to do research.

RELATE: Six related topics are presented to extend and enhance knowledge. These can be used for additional in-depth study.

As additional resources become available, a current resource list can be maintained in the classroom and updated periodically.

Completed projects can be displayed as part of an open house or research fair.

Animal Kingdom

READ:

The animal kingdom is a huge, diverse group of creatures. Animals come in all sizes, shapes, colorings, and markings. Their special traits and habits enable them to survive in their environments. Each is a creature unique to its own species. They roam the wild, can be tamed as pets, or visited in zoos or circuses. Some are in danger of becoming extinct if humans are not careful. They are an important part of the balance of life on planet Earth.

RESEARCH:

1. A biologist is a scientist who studies living organisms. Define each of the following specialists: entomologist, ichthyologist, conchologist, zoologist. What other '-ologists' are also involved in this field? Add them to the list.

2. What is your favorite animal? Why? Design a poster that describes its appearance, food source, habitat, location, and any unusual habits. Add illustrations to complete the research project.

3. Construct an "Animal Book of World Records." Set up pages for each of the animal record holders: best jumpers, fastest runners, smallest and largest in size. Come up with some other categories to add to your book. Which animals are the most unusual? Add a section for lesser-known animals, such as the mandrill, the wombat, the vicuna, the wallaby, and the ibex.

4. What might be some important rules for the treatment of animals? Develop an owner's manual of rules for the care and handling of pets. Visit a pet shop or your local animal shelter and interview the manager for tips pet owners can use. Design a poster of the rules and bring it to the pet shop for display!

RELATE:

Jane Goodall   ornithology   Carolus Linnaeus
zoology   endangered   U. S. zoos

Apples

READ:

People have been eating apples for thousands of years. Apple fossil remains have been found that date back about 5,000 years. Apples are grown worldwide. They are the most famous of all fruits, with more than 7,000 varieties available. Each apple variety looks and tastes different from one another.

RESEARCH:

1. According to the Bible, Adam and Eve ate an apple from the Tree of Knowledge and were expelled from Eden as a result. In what other stories or legends do apples play a central role? What do you think the apple represents in these stories?

2. Locate the U. S. Apple Association's Apple Usage Chart. According to their research, which apples are good for baking? Eating? Storing? Where are some of the major apple-producing regions? Prepare the information in an apple-shaped booklet. Display the booklet in the classroom when completed.

3. Do all apples have the same number of seeds? Cut several apples open and record the number of seeds. Note the apple variety. Do the same varieties have the same number of seeds? Do different varieties have different numbers of seed? When all experiments have been completed, create a seed design on art paper.

4. Create an apple collage. Cut out pictures and recipes related to apples and form them into an interesting collage. On one side of the design, brainstorm a list of all the tasty things you can think of that are made from apples.

RELATE:

Johnny Chapman   pomology   orchards
grafting   cider   *William Tell*

Architecture

READ:

Humans have always built a variety of structures to satisfy different needs. This involves thinking and visualizing in three dimensions, designing structures, detailed planning, and environmental considerations. From the cave dwellings of prehistoric France, to the huge pyramids of ancient Egypt, to the skyscrapers of today, there are no limits to the vision and creativity of structures people have erected. The great technological changes of the past 25 years have provided modern architects with wide freedom in the styles and materials used. Space created through the use of glass, fiberglass, decorative metals, and other materials provide many interesting options to architects today.

RESEARCH:

1. Create a list of the training and education needed to become an architect.
2. Define and illustrate the following architectural forms: arch, column, dome, and vault.
3. Pagodas, chateaus, chalets, and villas are structures used in different parts of the world. Read about these buildings and select one you would like to own someday. Explain why this would be your choice.
4. Examine the architectural style used for your home, school, or place of worship. What is the style of architecture used? What other buildings are similar?
5. Select any three world-famous structures from the list below and make a Structure Scrapbook. Include the location, date constructed, and intended purpose for each selection. Add illustrations and other architectural facts for your chosen structures.

Taj Mahal	Hermitage	Empire State Building
Eiffel Tower	Parthenon	Louvre
Coliseum	St. Peter's Cathedral	

RELATE:

Frank Lloyd Wright	I. M. Pei	Mies van der Rohe
Eero Saarinen	Pyramids	Walter Gropius

© Mark Twain Media, Inc., Publishers

Astronomy

READ:

> You will behold a host of stars which escape the unassisted sight, so numerous as to be almost beyond belief!
>
> — Galileo

Astronomy is the oldest science and one that has fascinated humankind from the first time people looked up and observed the heavens. Today, scientists are preparing to explore Mars and beyond. The universe is being studied with the accumulated knowledge of years of launches. The vastness of space and its objects become more familiar with each probe. Millions and billions of miles from Earth are beginning to seem within reach in the future of space exploration programs.

RESEARCH:

1. Set up an astronomy card file. Define the following: supernova, quasars, comets, meteors, asteroids, neutron stars, black holes, cosmic rays, and the Van Allen belt. Add other terms and information to the file as you find them.
2. Many great scientists have added to our knowledge of astronomy. Write a few sentences about the discoveries of each of the following: Sir Isaac Newton, Nicolaus Copernicus, Johannes Kepler, Edmund Halley, and Edwin Hubble. Create a card for each scientist and put it in the file.
3. Powerful telescopes enable us to observe objects and events in space. Find out about the Mount Palomar telescope in California. Design a poster that illustrates the main features of this telescope.
4. Is there life elsewhere in space? This is a question that tantalizes scientists. What do you think? Why? Write at least two paragraphs about this. Research to find evidence to back up your argument.

RELATE:

photosphere umbra
light years   spectrum
sunspots   solar eclipse

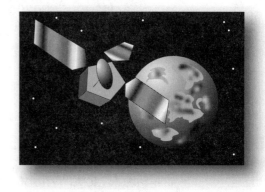

© Mark Twain Media, Inc., Publishers

Authors

READ:

Humankind has been telling stories for thousands of years. Literature is a record of experiences and patterns of life as told through the imaginations of authors and poets. Life is interpreted for the reader through the printed word. We enter the author's world, seeing imaginatively through his or her eyes.

Born and raised in Bombay, India, Rudyard Kipling (1865–1936) was sent to England by his parents for his education. At 17, he returned to India and began to write articles for many of the Anglo-Indian publications. Using his appreciation of the art and culture of India, his short stories about common people and soldiers of the British Empire gained popularity. He wrote about their lives using creative language that is memorable to this day.

RESEARCH:

1. Authors frequently use children as heroes or heroines in works of fiction. Compare the characters created by Charles Dickens, Louisa May Alcott, and Johanna Spyri. Explain how they are alike and different.
2. Read "How the Camel Got His Hump" by Kipling. It is light and humorous. Write a new ending for it.
3. What is a literary classic? Use a dictionary to define this term. What would you consider a classic today? Explain your choice.

BY RUDYARD KIPLING

4. Prepare a list of any five Newbery and/or Caldecott award winners you have read through the years. Which have been the most memorable? Why? Prepare an advertisement to encourage others to read your choices.
5. Use the *Junior Book of Authors* or *Something About the Author*. Choose an author that had an interesting life that helped him or her write a book you like. How do you think that author's life impacted his or her story?

RELATE:

poetry	literary genres	illustrators
publishing	Library of Congress	copyrights

Aviation

READ:

Even in the earliest years, humans observed birds and were fascinated by their flight across the skies. From the Greek myth of Icarus, who flew too close to the sun and melted the wax of his wings, to Leonard da Vinci, who in 1492 drew blueprints for what would become the helicopter, the prospect of flight has captivated the imaginations of people everywhere. The earliest attempts to fly were often disastrous for inventors. But these failures did not deter others. Instead, interest in flight continued to motivate inventors who created structures that eventually evolved into the machines we have today.

Flight has caused the world to seem to shrink in size so that one can fly half-way around the world in a matter of hours. A trip from New York City to Los Angeles, an expensive trip that would have taken days in a car or on a train before commercial flight, now takes just under four hours and costs a few hundred dollars. This "shrinking" of the world has led to not only increased tourism, but a greater sharing of cultures and, more importantly, businesses and merchandise.

RESEARCH:

1. Define the following list of basic terms used in flight: lift, drag, friction, and gravity. Add a labeled diagram to illustrate each term.
2. Who was Bernoulli? What were his discoveries? Write a brief report about his life and contributions to the field of aviation.
3. Construct a time line of flight showing the major events in the development of aviation. Were there any attempts at aviation before da Vinci's proto-helicopter?
4. Charles Lindbergh and Amelia Earhardt were two of the earliest pilots to make record-setting flights. Read about their achievements and draw a map showing the flight path of each.
5. Greek mythology includes stories about Pegasus. What was this creature? What unusual ability did it have? Read about the mythological creature and write a summary about what it represented.

RELATE:

Hindenburg	aeronautics	ballooning
hang gliding	NASA explorations	the Wright brothers

© Mark Twain Media, Inc., Publishers

Biography

READ:

A biography presents an account of a person's life. It is written or told by another person. It can be about any person, living or dead, who accomplished something unusual or special. Biographies can be about explorers, presidents, authors, inventors, scientists—anyone who an author thinks might be important for others to know about.

RESEARCH:

1. Select a person you would like to know more about. Find out about their birth, their educational background, family life, and accomplishments. Write a short biography. Add illustrations to your work.
2. Use *The American Book of Days* and make a list of famous people who share their birthdays with you. Select one to read about. Prepare a three-minute talk about your findings to share with the class.
3. Start a biographical record of a family member. List things that happened to that person in the past, things that person is doing now, and things that person would like to do in the future. Add anything unusual or funny that has happened to your relative. Add some photographs showing that person at different ages.
4. Some biographies are unauthorized. What does that mean? How might an unauthorized biography differ from an authorized one? Can you find examples of both kinds?

RELATE:

autobiography	Hall of Fame	Kitty Kelly
Martin Luther King, Jr.	Lassie	Presidents

© Mark Twain Media, Inc., Publishers

Bones

READ:

The skeletal system is an important system in the body. Although bones seem hard as rock, they are actually living tissues that can repair themselves from damage, just like skin. Made up of bones, joints, and connective tissues, the skeletal system provides shape and substance for every movement. Taking care of this system of living tissues is an important part of healthy growth and development.

RESEARCH:

1. Define and explain the following skeletal terms: ligament, joint, cartilage, vertebrate, and invertebrate.
2. Save a bone from a meal. Clean the bone and let it dry for several days. Carefully cut the bone in half with an adult's help. What does the interior of the bone look like? What does this tell you about the animal it came from? Do you think your bones are similar or different from this bone?
3. How many bones are in the human body? How many are in a giraffe's body? A snake's? A fish's? A worm's? What do you think the number of bones an animal has tells us about that animal?
4. What are calcium and calcification? Prepare a brief summary of each term.
5. Create a word search using skeletal system words. Be sure to include a word key. Pass out your search to other students. Can they find all your words?

RELATE:

osteoarthritis   fractures   rickets
osteology   orthopedics   marrow

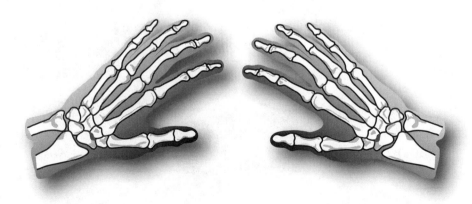

Botany

READ:

Botany is the science of plants. Their greenery and flowers brighten the world by adding color to the landscape. They are an important part of celebrations and holidays. But perhaps even more importantly, they are a vital source of food and medicines, and plants even help produce the oxygen we breath. You may not know that day lilies have been grown in China since ancient times for their culinary and medicinal uses, or that roses have been in cultivation for over 5,000 years. Did you know that secret messages were hidden in the carnation's large calyx, or outer covering, during the French Revolution? Or that calendulas were sent to France during World War I to be made into ointment for wounded soldiers? How about the dogwood being so named because it was used to make a folk remedy to help rid dogs of fleas? These beautiful blossoms are an important part of our history and culture.

RESEARCH:

1. What is your state flower? What does it symbolize? Display your findings on a poster.
2. Flowers are associated with the months of the year. Find the flower for your birth month and construct a labeled diagram of it.
3. *The Farmer's Almanac* has the following gardening hints: kill weeds by spraying them with white vinegar; combine equal amounts of water and skim milk and spray on roses to stop the fungal disease known as black spot; cover garden soil with spruce needles to keep cats away. Which of these hints really work? Which don't? Call a local agricultural agent and conduct an interview.
4. With permission from the teacher, arrange a field trip to a local florist. View the major tools used, seasonal flowers available, and techniques of floral arrangement.

RELATE:

giant sea kelp   terrace farming   poisonous plants
giant fern forests   root systems   medicinal herbs

© Mark Twain Media, Inc., Publishers

Bridges

READ:

Bridge has many meanings. It might be a card game, a raised platform on a ship, a structure used to cross water, or a movement from one period of time to another. It is those that cross bodies of water that are the most interesting to us here. Bridges have been used since ancient times and are usually a spectacular feat of engineering. Many are famous, such as the Golden Gate Bridge in San Francisco, California, and the Brooklyn Bridge in New York City. Bridge designers and builders need special educational backgrounds and training to accomplish the task of erecting a bridge.

RESEARCH:

1. Compile a listing of bridges that fit into these categories: longest, oldest, first of its kind, highest, most unusual, and most beautiful. Explain each type of bridge and where it is located. Keep all the activities from this project to form a Bridge Book to share with classmates.
2. Look at illustrations and explanations of bridges. Construct a three-dimensional model of one type of bridge. Upon what did you base your model?
3. Invite someone from an engineering firm to be a guest speaker for your class on the topic of bridges. Have questions prepared in advance. Don't forget to send a thank-you note afterwards!
4. Create a dictionary of the following bridge terms: truss, cables, arch, cantilever, tower, beam, and swinging. Include illustrations.
5. Some bridges are named to commemorate a person or place, such as the George Washington Bridge. Find a commemorative bridge and write a brief report about it.

RELATE:

John Roebling   Joseph B. Strauss   London Bridge
Bridge of Sighs   aqueducts   Golden Gate Bridge

Careers

READ:

What does a court reporter do? How might someone become an oculist? What is involved with becoming a franchisee? These are some of the many career areas available. As a person considers their likes and dislikes, special interests, and talents, they can see the interesting career choices available to them. Career choices expand as new technology develops and new discoveries are made. The career areas of today might be completely different in ten or 20 years. Careful planning and investigation are needed to match a career choice to current trends and personal qualities.

RESEARCH:

1. Make a list of three career areas that interest you. Check the classified ads in the newspapers for a week. How often are openings listed for the careers you chose? What are the qualifications? What kind of education is required?
2. Use your imagination and create an unusual career for the year 2050. It might be servicing the Space Shuttle as passengers travel to and from the moon, or even Mars! Create and write a want ad for a futuristic career.
3. Consult the current *Occupational Outlook Handbook*. How might this resource help with occupational decision-making? Write your opinion of this resource.
4. What is your dream career? Think about how you could attain this. Write a list of several goals you would need to achieve to fulfill your dream.
5. Visit sites where you can observe and interview people working in various careers. Have questions prepared in advance. What did you learn about those jobs? Write a brief summary of each job.

RELATE:

professional organizations   résumés   career trends
vocational education   unions   aptitude tests

© Mark Twain Media, Inc., Publishers

Caves

READ:

The forces of nature are constantly at work on Earth. While we can see what nature is creating above ground, did you know that below ground, amazing natural sights are also being formed? The forces of erosion and earth shifts have formed vast networks of caverns around the world. Their dark and mysteriously twisting paths have led to the creation of cave explorers, known as spelunkers, who enjoy the exploration of these sites as a hobby. One of the most famous cave areas in the world is the Lascaux Caves in France. Besides the unique cave features found there, one of the earliest examples of cave art was discovered there.

RESEARCH:

1. Find out more about the Lascaux Caves. Present a three-minute talk about them to your class.
2. Define these cave terms: stalactite, stalagmite, and limestone formations. Can you come up with an easy way to remember the definitions?
3. Create a travel brochure for visitors who would like to visit Mammoth Cave, Carlsbad Caverns, or Mount Rainier National Park Ice Caves. Locate each on a map and explain their most outstanding features.
4. Plants and animals that live in caves must adapt to the damp, dark environment. Create a poster showing a variety of these subterranean creatures. Identify each creature and write a short summary of how they adapted to living in caves.
5. Construct an interior cave view using a shoe box. Be sure to label the special cave formations.

RELATE:

stratigraphy
mineralogy
Mark Twain Cave
aquifers
geologic surveys
Mohs' Hardness Scale

© Mark Twain Media, Inc., Publishers

Chemistry

READ:

Every single thing that we see and feel, even those things we can't, is constructed of atoms. These extremely tiny, complex building blocks of life are similar in some ways to our solar system. Atoms are composed of large, heavy 'suns,' called nuclei. A nucleus is made up of protons and neutrons. Around the nucleus, electrons orbit in all directions, much like planets orbit around the sun. The identity of an atom depends on the number of protons in the nucleus. There are over a hundred elements, such as iron and helium, that are identified by the number of protons in their nuclei. We keep track of these elements on the Periodic Table of the Elements. Chemistry is the science of these elements and their interactions.

RESEARCH:

1. The physical state of all substances changes with temperature. Depending on the degree of heat, four states of matter are produced. Create a poster that defines each state and provides an example: solid, liquid, gas, and plasma.
2. The air that surrounds us is made from different gases. Cold temperatures bring the atoms that make up these gases closer together. Hot temperatures drive them farther apart. Blow up a balloon and weigh it. Then put that balloon in the refrigerator for 30 minutes and weigh it again. What do your findings tell you? Use the words *expand* and *contract* to describe your conclusions.
3. When we talk about energy, we describe it in two ways: potential and kinetic. Define these terms and devise an experiment to illustrate the difference between them. Demonstrate this experiment for the class.
4. What is Boyle's Law? Write a summary about his life and contributions to chemistry.

RELATE:

Paracelsus   anti-matter   crystallography
Democritus   Marie Curie   Enrico Fermi

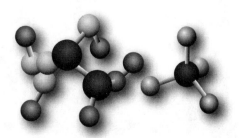

© Mark Twain Media, Inc., Publishers

Circus

READ:

The word *circus* is from the Latin word *kirkos*, which means 'circle' or 'ring.' The Roman circus was used for chariot races. The first modern circus was held in London, England, in 1770 and was later brought to America. In 1871, the best-known circus belonged to Phineas T. Barnum. It was known as "The Greatest Show on Earth." Barnum hired people who had unusual talents and abilities. He also incorporated animals, such as the giraffe, elephant, and chimpanzee, that Americans had never seen before. He later joined with another prominent circus, the Ringling Brothers circus. By 1919, the Ringling Brothers, Barnum and Bailey Circus was the biggest and best circus around. The long and colorful history of this circus is preserved today in a museum in Sarasota, Florida. This museum displays circus artifacts, biographies of famous circus performers, and chronicles of the history of the circus.

RESEARCH:

1. Make a booklet that lists all the things that can be found at a circus. Be sure to include illustrations. Make an outline of a large circus tent on art paper for the cover.
2. There are many performers in a circus: trapeze artist, juggler, lion tamer, acrobat, ringmaster, and clown, among others. Choose a famous performer that interests you and write a brief biography. Be sure to include photographs or illustrations of your chosen performer performing.
3. Imagine what it might be like to work in a circus. What job would you do? Write a poem about your role in a circus.
4. Circus clowns are highly trained performers. Did you know that there is an actual clown college? Research this college and write a brochure advertising its features to a potential applicant. What are some of the classes offered? What are some specializations available?

RELATE:

Emmett Kelly   Clyde Beatty   Frank Buck
Joseph Grimaldi   the Wallendas   Dumbo

Color

READ:

> I never saw a purple cow,
> However I hope to see one;
> But I can tell you anyhow,
> I'd rather see than be one!
> — Gelett Burgess

What would the world be like without color? There are geologic features named for colors; different cultures use colors to convey power and wealth; authors and artists use colors to give life to their creations; colors can reflect and even change our moods. But what is color? Color is pigment. All colors are based on the primary colors, which are red, blue, and yellow. In addition to black, which is all colors combined, and white, which is the absence of color, the complete range of colors we see can be made from the primary colors.

RESEARCH:

1. Experiment with color. Using watercolor paint, mix each of the following pairs of colors and record what color the combination produces. Blue and yellow, black and red, red and yellow. Experiment with other colors and record your findings. What was your favorite color?
2. Define the following color terms: hue, brightness, saturation, tint, and color wheel. Create a poster that illustrates the differences between these terms.
3. School colors are an important part of a school's tradition. What do your school colors signify? Design a new T-shirt for your school using the school colors.
4. Different colors mean different things to different people. What does the color red stand for in China? Why did kings and queens wear purple robes? Why does the U. S. President live in the White House? Why is blue associated with boys and pink with girls in so many countries? Has that always been true?
5. *Sunflowers* is a painting by Vincent Van Gogh. It is a brilliant study of yellows. Find a picture of this painting and study it. How does it make you feel? Write a short poem using at least five adjectives describing your emotions.

RELATE:

Little Boy Blue	Red Sea	color blindness
rainbows	*The Wizard of Oz*	Andy Warhol

© Mark Twain Media, Inc., Publishers

Communication

READ:

In the mid 1800s, America was beginning an unprecedented expansion westward. As new cities, like San Francisco, California, sprang up and enlarged in response to the discovery of gold, it became apparent that a speedier means of communicating from east to west was needed. So to replace the slow, unreliable system of mail carried on stagecoaches, the Pony Express  was born. Horseback riders were hired to ride day and night, sometimes through unsettled, often dangerous parts of the country. Using a system of relay stations located every ten to 15 miles, the Pony Express became the fastest way to send mail out west. Originating in St. Joseph, Missouri, riders could travel as many as 70 miles a day. The first trip, over 1,966 miles long, was accomplished in a record 10 days.

RESEARCH:

1. Relay stations provided food, rest, and a change of horses to the Pony Express riders. Write a diary page as a rider who has just stopped for the night at a relay station. Describe your day riding for the Pony Express. What did you see? How far did you travel? How many stops did you make?

2. Americans often design stamps to commemorate important events or people. Design a commemorative stamp honoring the brave Pony Express riders. What are some important features to include in your stamp to help people remember the Pony Express?

3. The Pony Express gradually ended when a new telegraph system was completed. Construct a booklet detailing the construction of the telegraph system and explaining why it led to the demise of the Pony Express. Be sure to include illustrations.

4. Many other cultures have used horses and riders to transport messages. What are some other ways people have sent messages? Construct a time line illustrating which group used what method to send information.

RELATE:

Bill Hickcock   William Cody   Western Union
transcontinental railroad   Morse code   Bronco Charlie Miller

Continents

Continents

READL:

It is believed that the land on Earth started as one landmass called Pangaea. Slowly, the landmass broke apart and individual continents took shape. Today, the seven continents are Asia, Africa, Antarctica, Australia, Europe, North America, and South America. With the exception of Antarctica, which has no native human population, each continent has a number of countries contained within it. Africa has 53 countries, Asia has 49, Europe has 47, North America has 23, and South America has 12. Australia is unique in that it is the only continent that is also a single country. The continent with the largest population is Asia, with over 60 percent of the world's people living on approximately one third of the world's land. Australia has only 0.5 percent of the world's population, even though it has over 5 percent of the world's land.

RESEARCH:

1. Select a continent for study. Set up a chart and record major cities, noted geologic features, main products exported, and interesting sites to see.
2. Define these geographic features: sea, valley, waterfall, glacier, steppe, and desert. Make a sketch for each definition.
3. What is the lowest place in the world? Where is it located? How far below sea level is it? What is the highest place in the world? Where is it located? How high above sea level is it? What are the lowest and highest places in America?
4. What is the smallest country in the world? What makes it different from other countries? What is the largest country? How many people live there? Draw a map that compares the two countries' sizes in scale.
5. Which continent would you like to visit? Why? Create a brochure that advertises the features that interest you the most and share it with the class.

RELATE:

peninsula   plate tectonics   continental drift
ocean   continental shelf   fault lines

© Mark Twain Media, Inc., Publishers

Cowboys

READ:

Stories about the American cowboy are known worldwide. These iconic figures were the mainstay of a way of life that has been romanticized in literature, art, and film. In reality, the cowboy era covers a brief period of about 30 years beginning after the Civil War ended. In 1865, the western frontier was mostly open plains, suitable for ranching. Cowboy work was hard, dirty, and dangerous. As the West became more settled and railroads connecting the country were built, less space for cattle grazing was available. Slowly, the vast space once inhabited by the cowboys and their cattle was replaced with farms, towns, and cities, and the cowboy way of life disappeared.

RESEARCH:

1. Every article of clothing cowboys wore was important. The wide-brim hat was a protection against the weather and could be used to carry water or wave signals. What was the importance of chaps, pointed boots, vests, and stirrups? Explain each item's role in a cowboy's life and use illustrations to make a poster.

2. Imagine a trail drive that was out more than a month herding cattle to market. Several thousand cattle needed to be watched over as the herd made its way to its final destination. A cowboy's food consisted of beans, biscuits, canned or dried fruit, jerky, and whatever fresh meat they could hunt. Write a diary entry about what you think it would have been like to be a cowboy riding with the herd.

3. Bill Pickett was the first African-American in the Cowboy Hall of Fame. He invented *bulldogging*, a way to wrestle a steer to the ground. Explain what bulldogging was.

4. Many of the skills cowboys used live on today in rodeos. What happens at rodeos today? What are some of the events featured? Write a short report on rodeos and present it to the class.

RELATE:

Gene Autry	Santa Fe Trail	Chisholm Trail
cow towns	gauchos	"Home on the Range"

© Mark Twain Media, Inc., Publishers

Culture

READ:

In the early 1900s, America was called the great melting pot as immigrants poured into the country from Europe. Thousands came to find new opportunities and a better way of life. Some were leaving behind political or religious oppression. But they all shared the desire to become Americans. Immigrants continue to come to America, although they now come from every country in the world. As our population grows and becomes a global mixture of cultures, people's perspectives change as they learn about each other's backgrounds and experiences.

RESEARCH:

1. Look at the month of December on a calendar. What are the different holidays celebrated by different cultures and religions during this month? Set up a chart to show the following for each holiday: country of origin, celebration customs, special foods used, and participating groups. Add illustrations showing important symbols for each holiday.
2. Interview classmates about their cultural heritage. Create a booklet that showcases the cultural background of all the students and illustrates important customs, dress, and foods for each group.
3. Imagine that it is 1912. You have just arrived in America from Europe. You have crossed the Atlantic by yourself. You do not speak English and have little money to spend. Write a letter home to your family describing your journey and experiences.
4. Investigate the *Encyclopedia of World Culture* by David Levinson. For what would you use this book? Describe one interesting feature about this source and how you would use it.

RELATE:

Ellis Island   immigration laws   citizenship
naturalization   Statue of Liberty   asylum

Deserts

READ:

Death Valley, on the border between California and Nevada, is the lowest, hottest, and driest place in the United States. It is about 140 miles long. More than 80 miles of its basin lies below sea level. Bitter salt pools simmer beneath the scorching sun. An average of one and a half inches of rain falls annually, and some years, no rain falls at all. The Saguaro cactus is one of the few things that can survive in this desolate place. It can grow to a height of 50 feet and can weigh up to six tons.

RESEARCH:

1. Write a brief report about Death Valley. Include information about how it got its name, how it was formed, what animal and plant life exists there, and what people have mined there. Present your findings to the class.
2. The largest living things in American deserts are the Saguaro cacti. However, there are many other varieties of cacti, including some, like the Saguaro, that flower. Select three varieties that you find unusual. Draw an illustration of each and explain how they are unique.
3. Make a poster illustrating how cacti can be used. Make sure to include both how people use cacti and how animals use cacti.
4. Deserts can be found around the world. Find any five deserts and draw a map showing the location of each one.

RELATE:

Painted Desert
oasis
mirage
Bedouins
gila monsters
dromedary camel

Dinosaurs

READ:

We can only imagine the magnitude of the giants that once roamed Earth many years ago during the Jurassic period. Only 200 years ago, however, dinosaurs were virtually unheard of. It wasn't until the 1800s that scientists and archeologists began finding the remains of these creatures. In 1822, the remains of a 15-foot-high creature called Iguanodon were found, and by the late 1800s, more than 130 different skeletons had been discovered. Today, over 900 different dinosaurs have been named. Many have been on display at various universities and museums. It is an awesome experience to see these reconstructed ancient creatures firsthand.

RESEARCH:

1. Carnivores are meat-eating animals, herbivores are plant-eaters, and omnivores eat a combination of both. Design a chart that lists three dinosaurs for each group. Include the official dinosaur name, what it is commonly called, its approximate size, and its food source.

2. How would you compare a lion and a Tyrannosaurus rex? A rhinoceros and a triceratops? A giraffe and an apatosaurus? Create a poster that illustrates the differences and similarities between one of the pairs of animals.

3. Dinosaurs became extinct after ruling the earth for many years. What might have happened to cause such a huge group of land, sea, and air creatures to die? Brainstorm a list of ideas with a classmate. Which idea is most probable? Least probable? Compare your ideas to those of paleontologists.

4. Some people maintain that some dinosaurs evolved into birds. How are birds similar to what we know about dinosaurs? How are they different? Based on your findings, do you agree or disagree with this theory?

RELATE:

amber	fossils	geology
paleontology	Edward Cope	crocodiles

© Mark Twain Media, Inc., Publishers

Disasters

READ:

The forces of nature have always instilled fear and respect in humankind. People have used a variety of methods in an attempt to understand these awesome forces and cope with their consequences. Throughout the centuries, people have become more informed and skillful in using technology to predict natural events and practice preventative measures. While natural disasters still have the potential to wreak great havoc on people's lives, every event produces new opportunities to learn about both the prevention of future disasters and the strength of the human spirit.

RESEARCH:

1. Define the following terms: flood, tornado, earthquake, tsunami, hurricane, and volcano. Create a poster illustrating each type of disaster and where it is likely to occur.

2. The volcanic destruction of Pompeii was one of the worst natural disasters ever discovered. Write a brief summary explaining what happened to Pompeii and how this disaster helped archeologists today learn about life in ancient Rome.

3. Earthquake activity occurs over 50,000 times a year. What causes earthquakes? Where do earthquakes occur? Construct and label a diagram showing what happens to the layers of earth when an earthquake occurs.

4. The Indonesian tsunami of 2004 and Hurricane Katrina were two recent major natural disasters, each causing millions of dollars in damage and taking thousands of lives. Using the Internet, look up ten facts about each disaster and research what people are doing to prevent similar disasters from occurring in the future.

5. Investigate your school plan for coping with a natural disaster. Does it address the major risks in your area? What are some issues with which you think the plan needs to deal? Write a letter to the principal with your suggestions.

RELATE:

Richter Scale	Johnstown flood	Fujita Tornado Intensity Scale
Great Dust Bowl	Krakatoa	Tornado Alley

© Mark Twain Media, Inc., Publishers

Drama

READ:

> All the world's a stage
> — Shakespeare

Drama was first developed by the ancient Greeks. Believing that watching a dramatic play was cathartic, the Greeks used tragedy and comedy to help rid the audiences of bad feelings. The tradition of using masks to represent happiness and sadness in a play began with the Greeks as well. In the centuries since drama emerged as a public art form, every age has produced a playwright whose works have defined his time. From Shakespeare to Shaw to Miller, the works created by these playwrights have played an important part in people's lives. Theatre today is a creative experience, enriching the lives of performers and audiences from small-town high schools to Broadway.

RESEARCH:

1. Construct a model of a theatre stage. Label the stage parts and write a brief summary about the purpose of each one.
2. Shakespeare is considered by many to be the greatest playwright of all time. Create a poster illustrating the important events in his life and highlighting the major plays he wrote.
3. Research masks in drama. Were the masks used by the Greeks the same as the masks used to represent comedy and tragedy today? For what were the Greek masks used? Design a Greek mask and present a brief report to your class on how that mask would have been used.

4. Have you ever been to a live theatre performance? What play did you see? What was it like? Write a short informative report detailing your experience with the theatre.
5. Other cultures have forms of drama as well. What can you learn about kabuki theatre? How is it similar to ancient Greek theatre? How is it different?

RELATE:

commedia del' arte	Aeschylus	Broadway
Tennessee Williams	Andrew Lloyd Webber	morality plays

Energy

READ:

Energy surrounds us in many ways. Whether it is the electricity we use when turning on a light, the gasoline needed to power our cars, or the magnetism that holds our magnets to our refrigerator, energy is present in many different forms. Some forms of energy, such as solar energy, are renewable, while other forms, such as fossil fuels, are not. We live in an energy-consuming society. Scientists are constantly looking for new sources of energy and better ways to use the energy we already have.

RESEARCH:

1. What was life like before electricity was commonly available? Imagine what your day would have been like. How would you have gotten up on time in the morning? What would it have been like to prepare and preserve food? How would you have studied in school? Write a diary entry describing what your day would have been like.

2. Whether due to mechanical problems or bad weather, sometimes we lose power. How will you and your family cope with an energy emergency? List the steps you would take to get home, stay warm or cool, and prepare dinner. Be sure to include items, such as flashlights, that you would need to have easily available in a power outage.

3. Define the following energy terms: wind, solar, hydroelectric, gasoline, biofuels, nuclear, and natural gas. Which forms of energy are renewable? Which are non-renewable? What are the pluses of using one form of energy? What are the minuses? Design a poster that illustrates these energy sources and highlights the form of energy you think we should use.

4. Construct an oversized model of a battery. How does a battery work? Be sure to label the individual parts and explain their purposes.

RELATE:

Thomas Edison	Three Mile Island	ethanol
windmills	brownouts	horsepower

Food

READ:

Every person must eat to live. But in many cultures, food is more than just about survival. Food is one of the foundations of the human experience. Eating food can be part of a religious ritual, a family tradition, or a social event. The things people eat vary widely depending on their environments, local customs, and family traditions. People from different parts of the world prefer different flavors, textures, and ingredients. Diets of cultural groups interest scientists and health professionals. They try to determine how eating habits affect health and what makes some foods good for you and others bad. Whether you eat dal, escargot, or macaroni and cheese, food is an important part of your life.

RESEARCH:

1. Many foods we enjoy in America were borrowed from other cultures. Investigate the origins of pizza, fried rice, and burritos. Write a brief summary explaining where each food comes from, how they are prepared in their country of origin, and how they have been changed here in America.

2. The Food Pyramid is a guide to eating a healthy diet. Draw a labeled diagram of this structure showing the food groups for each section. Include some illustrations of the recommended foods.

3. Adults have about 10,000 taste buds. Experiment with foods that are sweet like candy, sour like lemons, salty like pretzels, and bitter like dark chocolate. Do these flavors seem stronger in one area of the tongue or another? Draw a map of your tongue to show which areas are associated with each flavor.

4. Pick one country from each continent (except Antarctica). What is a popular food in those countries? Do Americans eat a version of that food? Which one sounds the most appealing to you? Draw a poster illustrating the countries you chose and the foods eaten there.

5. Bread is a universal food. What are some of the forms of bread eaten around the world? Make a list of different kinds of breads and the countries from which they come.

RELATE:

| vitamins | Le Cordon Bleu | Julia Child |
| USDA | organic | calories |

Fossils

READ:

Throughout the long history of the earth, an amazing variety of plants and animals have lived and died. Sometimes, when a plant or animal died, its remains were covered in mud or sand, preserving them. These preserved

bones, forms, and shapes are known as fossils. Scientists have developed a special process known as carbon-14 dating to determine the age of fossils. Whether analyzing a dinosaur bone or a human skeleton, scientists are able to learn valuable information from fossils. Fossils can tell us about the environment at the time of death of the organism, whether the organism was male or female, what an animal or person ate, how old they were when they died, and what caused their death. Scientists are continually using fossils to build a more complete picture of the history of Earth.

RESEARCH:

1. The La Brea Tar Pits in Los Angeles, California, have provided scientists with a great deal of fossil information. What are the La Brea Tar Pits? How were they formed? Write a short report about this important site.
2. A living fossil is a plant or animal that has not changed much over the years. Some examples of living fossils include: cockroaches, ginkgo trees, starfish, sponges, and crocodiles. Create a booklet that highlights these and other living fossils. Be sure to include a brief summary about the living fossil, illustrations, and any relatives.
3. The Petrified Forest is a National Monument and a popular place for fossil viewing. Where is the Petrified Forest located? What makes this forest unique? Design a brochure for tourists to advertise the Petrified Forest. Be sure to include a brief history of the forest, a map of its exact location, and illustrations.

RELATE:

geology   Mary Anning   paleontology
coelacanth   Richard Owen   trilobite

Genealogy

READ:

Genealogy is the study of family histories. By researching birth, marriage, and death certificates; military records; land deeds; letters; family Bibles; and other family papers, it is possible to construct a chart of your family history. The largest collection of this type of information is the Mormon Family History Library in Salt Lake City, Utah. Information has been documented there from before 1900 on more than a million rolls of microfilm. Each year, over 30,000 new rolls are added. The Library also houses over 200,000 volumes of records for about 100 million names in the Genealogic Index.

RESEARCH:

1. Create a family tree for yourself. Can you trace back to your great-grandparents? Interview your parents and grandparents for information about your family. Try to find pictures of each family member you list. How big is your family tree?

2. Write for free information about researching your family to: The National Genealogical Society, Educational Division, 4527 17th Street North, Arlington, VA 22207-2399. What did you learn?

3. Technology is changing the way people study genealogy. DNA testing can now prove that two people are or are not related. Find out information on this topic and write a brochure advertising DNA testing to people researching their family history.

4. In England, royalty often use a coat of arms, or special symbol, to represent their family history. Design a coat of arms that highlights what makes your family special. What images will you use to symbolize your family's unique history?

RELATE:

| Ellis Island | National Archives | Mayflower |
| slave records | newspaper archives | Thomas Jefferson |

Geography

READ:

Geography is the study of people and the world in which they live. Geography helps us understand our world and our place in it. Geography is more than just maps that show us how to get from here to there. Geography investigates the culture of a group of people that live in a specific location and how their environment and beliefs shape their lives. When you learn about the politics, religion, traditions, dress, and food of a group of people, you are studying geography.

RESEARCH:

1. Imagine you are a researcher who discovered your town. How would you describe the geography of the place you live? Write a short report analyzing your town. Be sure to include descriptions of important landmarks, the people who live there, how they dress and act, and what they eat.

2. What can you learn about your state? Design a poster that includes a picture of your state and information such as population, major cities, history, important landmarks, and state symbols including the state bird, state flag, and state slogan.

3. Geography can help us understand world events. What important geographical event happened in Europe in 1989? How did politics, culture, and nationalities change as a result of this event? Write a brief summary that explains what happened.

4. Where is Lake Baikal (also spelled Baykal) located? What makes this lake special? Compare this lake to America's largest lake, Lake Superior. How are these two lakes similar? How are they different?

RELATE:

cartography   archipelago   Prime Meridian
Great Rift Valley   Prince Henry the Navigator   population density

Geometry

READ:

Geometry is the study of shapes, their properties, and relationships. The word *geometry* means earth (geo) and measure (metry). Geometry is present in every aspect of our lives. We can see geometry in action by looking at our houses, our dinner plates, our bicycles, even our pencils and papers. Whether we admire the shape of a flower or try on different styles of eyeglasses, geometry is impacting our opinions. When you study a pattern, notice similarities, or experience an optical illusion, you are using geometry.

RESEARCH:

1. Define the following geometry terms: theorem, proof, postulate, coordinates, symmetry, and congruence. Why are these important terms to know? Write a rhyming poem that explains these terms.
2. The Golden Ratio was a principle of construction used by ancient builders and architects. The principle produced visually pleasing architecture that can be seen in buildings such as the Parthenon in Athens, Greece. What was the Golden Ratio? Write a brief description and use an illustration of the Parthenon to help explain your findings.
3. Pythagoras, Euclid, and René Descarte were great mathematicians. Write a short paragraph about their lives and their contributions to the field of geometry.
4. Explore the works of M. C. Escher. How did he use geometry to create his unusual optical illusions? Can you draw an Escher-style building?
5. Investigate a Fibonacci Sequence. What is it? Where are Fibonacci Sequences found? Create a poster that explains a Fibonacci Sequence and include illustrations that demonstrate this principle.

RELATE:

Goldbach's Conjecture
The Giza Pyramids

Blaise Pascal
tessellation

tangrams
deductive reasoning

Great People

READ:

> If I have seen further, it is by standing upon the shoulders of giants.
> — Sir Isaac Newton

Who is a great person? What qualifies a person to be great? It depends on an individual's values and ideas. For some, what makes a person great might be the contributions that person made to society. Others might value a life of achievement in spite of great personal tragedies. A great person could be a family or community member; a great person could be a world-renowned figure. Admiring great people inspires us to follow in their footsteps.

RESEARCH:

1. Consult *Webster's Biographical Dictionary*. Choose someone who made great contributions to the fields of mathematics or science. Write a short report about the person's life and discoveries.

SIR ISAAC NEWTON

2. Alfred Nobel established the Nobel Prizes in Stockholm, Sweden. Every year, the Nobel Prize Committee awards the Nobel Prize to people who work to further the interests of humanity in such fields as peace, literature, and medicine. Who was the only female to ever receive the prestigious award twice? Find out about which category she won and what her discoveries were.

3. Who would you consider to be a local great person? Is there someone in your community who has made an important difference in your life or the lives of others? Write a short article informing your reader about this person and his or her special achievements or accomplishments. Submit your article to your local paper.

4. Most people have heard of the Baseball Hall of Fame in Cooperstown, New York. But did you know there is also a Bowling Hall of Fame? Or a Rock and Roll Hall of Fame? There are many Hall of Fame sites around the country. Research one and describe the type of people commemorated there.

RELATE:

| biography | autobiography | Mother Teresa |
| living organ donors | heroes | Canton, Ohio |

© Mark Twain Media, Inc., Publishers

Insects

READ:

Millions of insects inhabit Earth. Some have been around since the time of the dinosaurs. Others have yet to be discovered. While we may see insects as pesky or bothersome, they have an important place in our ecological system. Many are food sources for other animals. Some serve as environmental cleaners, breaking down waste or dead matter. Still other insects produce foods that humans value. Insects can vary in appearance from cute to ugly, funny to scary. Their actions can be irritating or humorous. Whether we love or loathe them, insects are an integral part of our world.

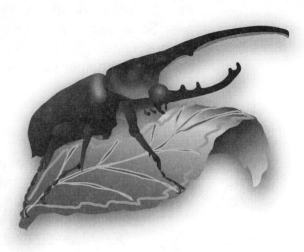

RESEARCH:

1. Invite a beekeeper or entomologist to speak to your class. Prepare questions in advance, and don't forget to send a thank-you note after the person's visit.
2. While insects can vary dramatically in appearance, they all have some parts in common. Draw a diagram of the insect body. Be sure to label the individual parts that all insects share.
3. Mosquitoes are an annoying part of summer. Their itchy bites drive many people and animals indoors at dusk. But mosquitoes have an important role in the food chain. Write a brief report on mosquitoes that examines their positive role in the environment. Be sure to include illustrations and a title.
4. You have heard sayings like "don't bug me" and "busy as a bee." What other insect-related sayings can you find? Start a bug phrase book. Add a fun illustration for each saying.
5. Honey comes from honeybees. What are some other insect-related foods people in a variety of cultures eat?

RELATE:

entomology	formicary	Dr. Walter Reed
walking stick	scarabs	insect camouflage

© Mark Twain Media, Inc., Publishers

Invention

READ:

From the bow and arrow in Neolithic times to the camera phone of today, new ideas and inventions have made life easier and safer for humankind. Whether it is a complex device, such as the microprocessor, or a simple thing, like Post-It Notes®, nearly everything we use was invented by someone in the past. Some inventors, such as Leonardo da Vinci or Thomas Edison, are quite famous. Others, such as the inventors of the wheel or shoelaces, may never be known. Whether famous or not, all inventors look for ways to improve the quality of our lives.

RESEARCH:

1. "Necessity is the mother of invention," is an old saying that illustrates the idea that people create what they need the most. If you could invent something to solve a current problem, what would it be? Describe your problem and what you would invent to solve it.

2. What did Chester Greenwood invent on a cold day in 1873? What happened to him after he began to sell his invention? Do you own one of his inventions? Write a short paragraph about his new idea and present it to the class.

3. Thomas A. Edison is famous for inventing the lightbulb, but he invented many more things. How many things did he invent? What are some of his other well-known inventions? Design a poster that provides a brief biography of Edison and illustrates some of his other inventions.

4. What do you consider the greatest invention of all time? Create a brochure that explains what makes that invention the greatest and persuades your readers to agree with you.

5. Interview one of your grandparents or another senior citizen. Ask them what life was like before such now-common inventions like the microwave, the remote control, the computer, or television. What did they do before these things were invented?

RELATE:

trademarks   U. S. Patent office
copyrights   Philo T. Farnsworth
Rube Goldberg   Alexander Graham Bell

Kites

READ:

While often considered a child's pastime today, flying kites has been a popular activity for thousands of years. It is believed that the first kites were large tropical leaves attached to thin vines flown by prehistoric people. Egyptian hieroglyphics had symbols for kites, and Malayan priests used them in religious ceremonies over 3,000 years ago. Chinese folklore tells of kites with bamboo pipes attached that, when flown at night, whistled and frightened enemies away. Today, kites provide fun for all ages and can be found in many colors, shapes, and sizes.

RESEARCH:

1. In 1752, Benjamin Franklin flew a kite during a thunderstorm. Why did he do this? What did he prove? Pretend you are Franklin and write a diary entry describing your experiment and what you learned.
2. Japan has several kite traditions. Kite Day is a special celebration. What can you find out about Kite Day? Create a poster that describes the purpose of Kite Day and how the Japanese celebrate it.
3. Design your own kite. Go to a store that sells kites or check out a book about kites, and see what shapes of kites are available. What do you think is the best shape or combination of shapes? Sketch your kite and then build it out of what you think are the best materials. How far can you get your kite to fly?
4. The American Kitefliers Association is located at 321 East 48th Street, New York, New York, 10017. What does this association do? What sort of events do they have? Write a letter requesting more information about their activities.

RELATE:

aeronautics	kite fighting	Wright Flyer
parafoils	aerodynamics	Bernoulli's Principle

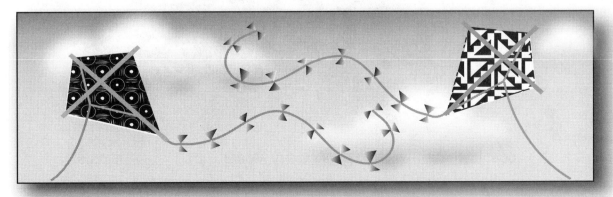

© Mark Twain Media, Inc., Publishers

Language Arts

READ:

Language arts are subjects, including reading, writing, spelling, and literature, that help people communicate with others. The English language is a complex, constantly evolving language. Its development can be traced back over thousands of years. From Chaucer's *Canterbury Tales* to Shakespeare's sonnets, from Charles Dickens' novels to the blogs of today, the language arts have helped unite people from different centuries and cultures with a greater understanding of the human spirit.

RESEARCH:

1. The English language includes many words that have been borrowed from other languages. Some, such as the Italian word *pizza* or the French word *chic*, seem obvious, but the origins of other words are less clear. Do you know where we get the word *skunk,* or what language *tycoon* comes from? Find out what some other borrowed words are. Create a poster that lists these words. Provide as many illustrations as you can.

2. *Slang* are new words or phrases that people use to express older ideas. Slang words lose popularity quickly and are frequently replaced by newer slang. Take the idea of *neat*, for example. From the 1950s to the present, slang words like *cool, groovy, bad, awesome, way cool,* and *phat* have been used to mean *neat*. Consult *The New Dictionary of American Slang.* What are some other slang words that have come and gone through the years? Come up with at least ten slang words that mean nearly the same thing.

3. The greatest library in the country is the Library of Congress in Washington, D. C. Investigate the Library. Create a brochure that includes information such as how many books the Library has, when it first began, how big it is, and other information. Be sure to include illustrations.

4. What is your favorite book? Write a short report to persuade other students to read your favorite book.

RELATE:

poet laureate   Newbery Medal   idioms
Samuel Johnson   storytelling   blogs

© Mark Twain Media, Inc., Publishers   34

Maps

READ:

Since ancient times, humans have used maps to show where they were and where they wanted to go. Early civilizations carved maps into clay or wood, while later, people painted maps onto parchment and then paper. In addition to knowing where they are, maps help people understand the world around them. Maps were valuable. Many maps were destroyed to keep information from falling into the wrong hands. Maps can tell us what the shape of the land is, where there is water, what the borders of a state or country are, or how many people live in an area. However, a map is only as good as the knowledge of the mapmaker. A map from 1,000 years ago is very different from a map only 100 years old, and neither map looks anything like a map created today. The maps we have today may not look anything like the maps made in 50 or 500 years as new cities are built, nations break apart and reunite, and geological shifts occur.

RESEARCH:

1. One of the earliest maps discovered is the amazing Piri Reis map. What does this map show? When and where was it found? Write a short paragraph explaining the history of this map. Be sure to include an illustration.
2. Define the following kinds of maps: Mercator, Homolosine, Lambert Equal-Area, Homolographic, and Conic Projection. Which map produces the best representation of the earth? What are the flaws of each type of map? Create a poster that illustrates each kind of map and highlights your choice.
3. Construct a detailed map of the route from your home to your school. Be sure to include a legend, a compass rose, major street names, and any notable features along the way.
4. What is the difference between a contour map and a political map? What information does each map provide? Make a list of the attributes of each kind of map.
5. Maps have been revolutionized by technology. Global Positioning Systems, or GPS, are now widely available. What is GPS? How is this technology being used?

RELATE:

Catalan Atlas	Landsat	Cantino Map
cartographers	Gerardus Mercator	Prime Meridian

© Mark Twain Media, Inc., Publishers

Mathematics

READ:

Mathematics is a universal language. No matter where you are, one plus one will always equal two. Mathematics conforms to set rules and procedures and is a precise way to express ideas in many aspects of life. Great mathematicians through the ages have explored and written about ideas that still remain the basis for calculations and theories used today. Albert Einstein could not have expressed his theory of relativity if there were not a fundamental body of knowledge that came first. It may be possible that if and when we make contact with alien life, math will be the language we use to communicate.

RESEARCH:

1. Trigonometry and calculus are advanced forms of mathematics. Define each and explain their main usage.
2. What is a googol? Can you write it out? What Internet web site borrowed its name from this term? Why did it choose that name?
3. Experiment with the following sequence: 111 x 111; 111 x 121; 111 x 131; 111 x 141. What amazing discovery can you make?
4. Where did we get the concept of mathematical zero? What did people use before mathematical zero?
5. What are quadrillions and quintillions? How do scientists write these large numbers?
6. One of the most famous mathematical equations in the world is $E = Mc^2$. Who came up with this equation? What does it stand for? What does it prove?

RELATE:

Sir Isaac Newton   Stephen Hawking   pi
Goldbach's Conjecture   magic squares   fuzzy logic

© Mark Twain Media, Inc., Publishers

Measurement

READ:

Nearly everything we do is measured in some way or another. We count the minutes until our favorite show comes on. We celebrate growing older by having birthday parties. We decide what to wear based on the temperature outside. We argue with our brothers and sisters over who got the bigger piece of cake. Parents use allowances to reward children for completed chores. We award medals to the fastest runners and swimmers. Measurement allows us to keep track of our world and see how it is improving.

RESEARCH:

1. From the earliest times, people have needed to measure things. They began by using parts of their bodies as a way to measure distance. Design a poster that defines hand, foot, yard, and cubit and illustrates where these terms originated.

2. What is geologic time? How is it measured? Construct a time line of the major geologic periods. How long would your life be on your geologic time line?

3. Area and perimeter are ways to measure the size of the space around us. Explain how each is calculated and give an example of when you would use area and perimeter.

4. Look through *The Guinness Book of World Records.* What are some of the most unusual records? Make a chart that identifies what was done, the year it happened, and the measurements that made it worthy of being listed in the book.

5. Light-years are a way of measuring distance in outer space. What is a light-year? How far away is the nearest star system, Alpha Centauri, in light-years? Create a brochure advertising travel to this star system.

RELATE:

Aztec calendar   blood pressure   statistics
U. S. Census   February 29th   metric system

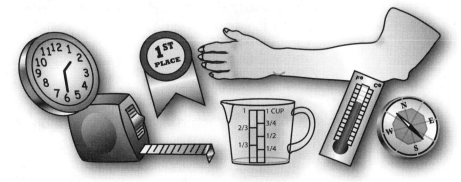

© Mark Twain Media, Inc., Publishers   37

Money

READ:

> A penny saved is a penny earned.
> — Benjamin Franklin

Money is a medium of exchange used to obtain goods and services. Money allows people to acquire what they need. The history of money is filled with interesting stories, legends, and myths. While we may think of money as coins and green bills, money has been different things to different cultures. The Iroquois tribe used a particular type of cowrie shell as money. Roman soldiers were paid in salt, giving us the word *salary*. Gold and silver, used as money for thousands of years, was one of the primary reasons conquistadors explored the New World. In 1934, the United States Treasury issued a $100,000 gold certificate with the former president Woodrow Wilson pictured on it. This was the highest denomination of paper currency ever issued in the world.

RESEARCH:

1. What is the euro? How much is it worth in American dollars? When did the European Union begin using it as legal currency? Design a poster that illustrates the euro and the forms of money the euro replaced.

2. Usually, presidents are featured on our money. However, there are a few exceptions. Create a brochure that lists every denomination of American money and who is featured on it. Which denominations do not feature presidents?

3. Visit a local bank. Talk with a bank representative and find out about a savings account. What is the minimum balance? How much interest would you earn? Would the interest be compounded? Make sure you understand these banking terms. If you do not already have one, open a savings account.

4. What is the lottery? Does your state have a lottery? What are the chances of winning a jackpot? What would probably give you more money: buying one lottery ticket every day, or saving one dollar every day in a savings account? How much would you have after 20 years?

RELATE:

U. S. Treasury	Denver Mint	New York Stock Exchange
barter system	J. P. Morgan	Monopoly™

© Mark Twain Media, Inc., Publishers

Monuments

READ:

Monuments are special structures built to commemorate important people or events. They serve to remind people about history. Monuments can be small signs by the side of the road or large structures the size of a house. One of the largest monuments in the world is Mt. Rushmore. This monument to four great presidents is an impressive tribute. Located in the Black Hills of South Dakota, Mt. Rushmore features the faces of George Washington, Thomas Jefferson, Theodore Roosevelt, and Abraham Lincoln carved into the side of a mountain. Each face is over 60 feet tall, with the eyes measuring 11 feet wide and noses over 20 feet tall. Work began in 1927 under the supervision of Gutzon Borglum and his son. It was completed in 1941, shortly after the elder Borglum's death.

RESEARCH:

1. West of Mt. Rushmore, another carving is being sculpted on a mountain. Korczak Ziolkowski, who died in 1982, began the gigantic task of carving the great Sioux warrior Crazy Horse into a mountain. Create a poster that illustrates the history of the Crazy Horse mountain. Include information on why Ziolkowski dedicated his life to this project, how long the carving has lasted, how much of the monument is completed, how much money it has cost so far, and how much more it will take to finish the job.

2. Some cities are known for their famous monuments. Choose one of the following monuments and create a brochure encouraging people to visit: The Statue of Liberty, New York City, New York; The Gateway Arch, St. Louis, Missouri; The Space Needle, Seattle, Washington. Be sure to include important information, such as who designed the monument, when it was completed, what it is commemorating, and how many people visit it every year.

3. Washington, D. C., is home to over 160 monuments and memorials. How many memorials can you list? What do they commemorate? What is the most unusual memorial?

RELATE:

Hoover Dam   the Alamo   Liberty Bell
Gettysburg Battlefield   Eiffel Tower   Giza Pyramids

© Mark Twain Media, Inc., Publishers

Music

READ:

Music is the art of combining sound into different forms that are pleasing to the ear. From the classic masterpieces to today's popular songs, music is an outlet for our creative spirit. What began as the rhythmic beat of clapping hands and stomping feet has evolved into the varied forms available to us today. With instruments as different as the mouth harp and the sitar, music is a part of every culture in the world. Whether you sing, play an instrument, or listen, understanding and enjoying music is part of being human.

RESEARCH:

1. Who is your favorite American composer? Use *Popular American Composers* to find a composer you like. Write a short report about the life and times of this person. How did the era he or she lived in influence his or her music? Be sure to list some of the pieces that composer wrote.
2. "Music soothes the savage beast," is a common saying that means music can calm people and animals down. What are some other music sayings? Make a poster listing as many music sayings as you can think of. Be sure to include explanations.
3. Interview the band or choral director at your school. Ask about the education and training necessary for this job. What are some other jobs that involve making music?
4. How has popular taste in music changed over the years? Compare the best-selling album from 1945 to 1975 to 2005. What do these changes tell you about American culture during these times?
5. Choose a foreign country, such as India or Nigeria. What is the popular form of music there? What kind of instruments do they use? How is it similar to or different from popular American music? Write a brief report and present your findings to the class.

RELATE:

Broadway
hip hop

Richard Wagner
lullabies

Gregorian Chants
the Happy Birthday song

© Mark Twain Media, Inc., Publishers

Mythology

READ:

Greeks created gods and goddesses to help explain the world around them. First conceived to help explain such natural phenomena as lightning and winter, the gods and goddesses came to also embody human nature. Far from perfect, these gods and goddesses fell in love, got angry, had arguments, and felt sorrow. The Greek mythology was so complete in explaining the known world that it was largely adopted by the Romans, who changed little but the names. The resulting body of mythology has survived thousands of years as a testament to the enduring nature of these creative people.

RESEARCH:

1. Every culture has a creation myth. How did the Greeks explain the origins of the earth? How is this similar to other creation myths, such as the Navajo creation myth or the Hindi creation myth?

2. Greek and Roman mythology plays an important role in astronomy. Create a poster that identifies the names of all the planets in our solar system, which gods and goddesses they were named after, and why. Include illustrations of each god or goddess along with their planet namesake.

3. Many myths served as warnings. Choose one of the following myths and identify the lesson it is communicating: Daedalus and Icarus, Midas, Sisyphus, and Phaethon. Rewrite the myth you choose in your own words. Be sure to include illustrations.

4. Select a mythological character who fell out of favor with the gods. Describe the punishment this character received. Was this a just punishment? How did this punishment affect the mortal humans?

5. The Parthenon in Athens was a spectacular temple. To whom was the temple dedicated? What happened to the Parthenon?

RELATE:

Zodiac signs   Nashville, Tennessee   Titans
Homer   Ovid   Elgin Friezes

Newspapers

READ:

> A free press is the unsleeping guardian of every other right that free men prize.
> — Sir Winston Churchill

We live in a world of vast and varied forms of print. Newspapers provide the public with coverage of all manner of events. There are over 2,000 daily newspapers and 9,500 weekly newspapers in the United States alone. Their goals are similar: to inform, educate, interpret, serve, and entertain. To meet these goals, a variety of news and features are reported.

RESEARCH:

1. Select a daily newspaper to examine. Who are the readers of this paper? What sections make up the newspaper? How does this newspaper serve its audience?
2. News stories answer the following questions: who, what, when, where, and why. Select a story from today's newspaper to read. How many of the five W's did this story answer? Was anything missing? Write a short paragraph detailing your opinion of the article.
3. Journalists are trained professionals who report the news. What are some qualities journalists should have? Make a word chart that includes all the necessary qualities and the meaning of each one.
4. What does the above quote from Winston Churchill mean? Explain the meaning of the free press and list examples of how a free press has changed history.
5. Letters to the Editor are an important part of a newspaper. Write a letter to the editor of your local paper. Make a proposal that would help your school, and put forth your arguments. Then send your letter and see if it gets published!

RELATE:

Joseph Pulitzer	Thomas Paine	William Randolph Hearst
photojournalism	John Peter Zenger	the fourth estate

© Mark Twain Media, Inc., Publishers   42

Numbers

READ:

> [The universe] cannot be read until we have learned the language and become familiar with the characters in which it is written.
>
> — Galileo

While mathematics is a global language, no one can speak it until they understand numbers. Numbers are everywhere. They are used in all countries and cultures. While they may not be pronounced the same way in different languages, their value remains unchanged. The value of ten is always ten. While most of us think of counting when we think of numbers, mathematicians are working with numbers and number systems in ways that contribute to everything from building faster computers to understanding the nature of the universe.

RESEARCH:

1. Define the following number terms: real numbers, whole numbers, natural numbers, rational and irrational numbers, integers, and ordinals. Create a chart that shows how these terms can be similar and what the differences are among these types of numbers.

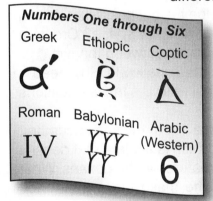

2. Number patterns are fun to compute. Try this: using the three table, multiply each number by 37. Start with 37 x 3, 37 x 6, 37 x 9, etc. What astonishing discovery can you make? Make a set of flash cards to use with family and friends. You can magically give the answers without any computation.

3. Counting to ten is one of a child's first experiences with numbers and language. In how many other languages can you count to ten? Design a poster that lists the words for each number in each language. Try to include five or more other languages.

4. "As I Was Going To St. Ives" is a well-known eighteenth-century rhyme. Find a copy of the poem and read it carefully. Can you calculate how many were going to St. Ives? Draw pictures to help solve the riddle.

5. Pi is an irrational number. What can you find out about pi? What is the symbol for pi? How many digits has it been calculated to? What is it used for? How far out can you calculate pi by yourself?

RELATE:

Pascal's Triangle	Napier's Rods	magic squares
scientific notation	googol	Charles Babbage

© Mark Twain Media, Inc., Publishers

Oceanography

READ:

Over three-fifths of the earth's surface is covered with water. In addition to the hundreds of seas, lakes, and rivers, the oceans are the Pacific, Atlantic, Indian, and Arctic. Beneath the water's surface, the ocean floor has many of the same features as the land. Mountains and canyons cross the ocean floor. The oceans are a wealth of resources for people. The floor is mined for natural gas and oil. The water is purified to make it drinkable. The plant and fish life provide people with food. The oceans' vast waters affect the weather and climate while also providing a variety of recreation. However, much of the oceans' mysteries remain undiscovered. Oceanographers are continually exploring the world's oceans to discover new and interesting information to better humankind.

RESEARCH:

1. Define the following ocean terms: tides; waves; currents; estuaries; euphotic, disphotic, and aphotic zones; and benthic realm. Make a brochure that explains these terms to a tourist. Why would these terms be good for a tourist to know?
2. Scientists use the term *inner space* to describe the oceans. What do you think this term means? How does it compare to *outer space*? Create a chart that explains the similarities and differences between the two.
3. The Mariana Trench is one of the deepest points in the world. How deep is it? Where is it located? Write a brief report that answers these questions and others about this underwater formation.
4. There is a wide variety of animal life in the sea. From the sea cucumber, which isn't a vegetable, to the whale shark, which is a shark that doesn't eat animals, there are some truly unusual creatures in the oceans. What are some of the more unusual creatures who make the oceans their home? Design a poster that illustrates what you think are the oddest creatures in the sea, and include a brief description of what makes these animals different.
4. The *Titanic* is one of the most famous shipwrecks in the world. Where is the wreck of the *Titanic* located? How do researchers study it? What sorts of things do they study? Write a short story about what a researcher does on the wreck of the *Titanic* and what they find.

RELATE:

Jacques Cousteau
kelp forests

The *Aquarius*
cold seeps

Great Barrier Reef
Hadal zone

© Mark Twain Media, Inc., Publishers

Optical Illusions

READ:

Do your eyes play tricks on you? They can when you are looking at an optical illusion. Optical illusions can be strange, baffling, and amazing. Color, size, and line length all play a part in creating an optical illusion. It all depends on the visual perception of the view and the ability to measure accurately what is seen. Optical illusions have a variety of uses. Artists have been creating optical illusions for thousands of years. Interior decorators use optical illusions to make rooms look bigger. Magicians use optical illusions to perform seemingly impossible tricks. You may have even used optical illusions to make yourself look older, taller, or thinner. Tricking how the eye sees the world may be a bigger part of your life than you realize!

RESEARCH:

1. The art of M. C. Escher, Piet Mondrian, and Paul Klee includes illusionary works. Explore and compare their works. What kind of illusions did they produce? Imagine you are a newspaper art critic and write a review of the work of these artists. Select your favorite works and explain why you like them.

2. What are a thaumatrope and a stroboscope? Find out what they are and create them out of cardboard. Can you see the illusion each produces?

3. The french phrase *trompe l'oeil* literally means to 'trick the eye.' We often use this phrase when describing a painting that makes it appear that objects, such as curtains, are in a room when in fact, they have been painted on the wall instead. Can you find an example of this kind of *trompe l'oeil*? Who created it? When was it painted?

4. Movies rely heavily on illusions to create a realistic story. For example, a movie may show a cold, snowy scene, but in reality, it might be 70 degrees outside, and the snow is potato flakes being shaken by crew members. Create a list of some common illusions and how movie makers trick us into believing them.

RELATE:

holograms	Cubism	depth perception
perspective	optics	David Copperfield

© Mark Twain Media, Inc., Publishers

Paper

READ:

Paper, used every day in hundreds of ways, was first invented over 1,900 years ago in China. Ts'ai Lun first made paper in the year A.D. 105 using

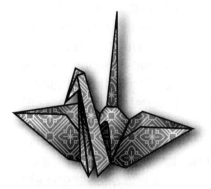

an assortment of material, including mulberries, bamboo fibers, fishing nets, and even rags. The Chinese emperor was so pleased with Lun's invention that he made Lun a member of the court. The process became a closely guarded secret for almost 1,000 years, until the Moors learned how to make paper and brought the idea to Europe. By the eleventh century, paper mills were springing up throughout Europe. Although still expensive, paper became more available. By the 1800s, wood pulp had become the primary ingredient in paper, making it affordable. Today, paper is a cheap, renewable, and recyclable product that many people take for granted.

RESEARCH:

1. Humans wrote on things long before paper was invented. What are some of the things people used before paper? Create a poster that illustrates what people used and how it was made. Find at least three writing surfaces to describe. Can you find five or more?
2. Johannes Gutenberg invented a printing press that used movable type in 1455. How did this change the use of paper? Research his life and describe his most important production in a short report.
3. Paper is made out of wood pulp. What are some other things that wood pulp can be made into? How many do you use on a daily basis?
4. Find an old document printed on paper from before 1920. What has happened to the paper? What steps can you take to preserve paper? Design a brochure that advertises some of the things you can do to keep paper from degrading.
5. Over 50 million tons of paper products are produced every year in the United States. How much paper does your class use? Collect all the paper products you used in a week and weigh it. How much did it weigh?
6. Recycling is an important activity. Why should you recycle paper? Do you recycle paper at school? At home? Find out about local recycling centers and start a recycling program at home or school. If one already exists, see how much paper you can recycle in one month.

RELATE:

quill pens   illuminated manuscript   *Medieval Book of Hours*
papier-mâché   bookworms   origami

Peanuts, Popcorn, Pizza!

READ:

Some of our favorite foods are packed with nutrition and are healthy to eat. Peanuts, popcorn, and pizza are all fun foods that we might eat while watching the game or hanging out with friends. Did you know that peanuts were grown about 2,000 years ago by ancient tribes in South America? Or that popcorn may have originated in Mexico more than 800 years ago? Or that Americans consume more than three billion pizzas every year? Even our afternoon snack and dinner has a long and interesting history!

RESEARCH:

1. In 1903, the first peanut butter machine was invented. Since then, peanut butter has become a staple of children's diets. But how many other products use peanuts? Imagine you work for the Peanut Association of America and create a brochure listing all the uses for peanuts.

2. Popcorn is a special type of corn. What are the three kinds of corn? What makes popcorn different from the other two? Why does popcorn pop? Design a poster that illustrates the kinds of corn and shows what happens to popcorn when it is heated.

3. According to *The Guinesss Book of World Records,* the largest pizza ever was baked in 1984 and was over 86 feet wide. Write a short newspaper article about this accomplishment. Who was involved? How was the pizza constructed? How much of the ingredients were used? How many pieces were cut?

4. The kind of pizza you eat often depends on where you live. New York style pizza is big and meant to be folded in two. Chicago pizza is about two inches thick, with the sauce on top of the cheese. St. Louis pizza is on a cracker-thin crust cut into squares. What other kinds of pizza are there? How is pizza different in other countries?

RELATE:

kettle corn
pizzerias

Jimmy Carter
pizza Margherita

George Washington Carver
Jiffy Pop®

© Mark Twain Media, Inc., Publishers

Poetry

READ:

I think that I shall never see / A poem lovely as a tree
— Joyce Kilmer

Poetry is a form of writing characterized by rhythm, line, and meter. It uses a language of image and emotion expressed by the poet. Poets use a variety of styles when writing poetry. Poetry can be a short, silly rhyme, such as a limerick, or long and story-based, like "Paradise Lost" by Milton. People enjoy poetry every day, although most poetry these days is in the form of song lyrics.

RESEARCH:

1. Haiku is a minimalist Japanese poetry style with three lines that follow a 5 / 7 / 5 syllable pattern. Basho was the most well-known haiku poet. Research the life and poetry of Basho. Create a poster that describes his life, and illustrate his poetry with one of his haikus. Can you write your own haiku?

2. Many people think poetry must be serious or boring, but Shel Silverstein proves otherwise. He wrote creative, imaginative poetry for children. Select one of his poems to memorize and perform in front of the class.

3. One of the most famous husband and wife poets were Robert Browning and Elizabeth Barret Browning. Research their lives. How did their story influence their poetry? How was their poetry similar? How was it different? Write a short report about their lives and poetry.

4. Poetry slams are a popular group activity. What are poetry slams? What do poets do at poetry slams? Organize a poetry slam for your classroom. Decide in advance how you will declare a winner and what the prizes will be.

5. Define the following poetic terms: iambic, cinquain, couplet, dactyl, anapest, and trochee. Can you find a poetic example for all of these words?

RELATE:

Emily Dickinson	the sonnet	shih
Dr. Seuss	Robert Frost	poet laureate

Presidents

READ:

Since 1789, when George Washington was elected the first president, citizens of this country have elected a leader every four years. Anyone born in America could grow up to be president. During this four-year term in office, the president is confronted with problems of national and international concern. The president has a Cabinet of advisors to help deal with issues. The president also works with Congress to pass laws. The president works and lives in the White House, located at 1600 Pennsylvania Avenue in Washington, D.C. There, the president meets with other elected officials, foreign leaders, and community members. The role of president is a varied, complex one that bears great responsibility.

RESEARCH:

1. The presidential oath of office is administered during the inaugural ceremonies by the chief justice of the Supreme Court. What is the oath the president must recite?

2. Presidential pets have been almost as famous as the presidents themselves. Starting with Franklin Delano Roosevelt, find out what pets the presidents have had. How many have had dogs? How many have had cats? Create a chart showing which president had which pet.

3. Many presidents have a library dedicated to their lives and times in office. Visit the web site of a presidential library. What types of exhibits does the library offer? What is the cost of admission? Design a brochure for tourists encouraging them to visit the presidential library you choose.

4. One of the many duties of the president is being the commander-in-chief. What responsibilities does this title bring? How many presidents were actually military leaders in the years before becoming president? In what wars did they fight?

5. Presidents have always had campaign slogans as part of their election campaigns, such as "Tippecanoe and Tyler Too." Find out what some of the more memorable campaign slogans have been. Do you think they worked to get their candidates elected?

RELATE:

Mount Vernon	executive branch	Monticello
electoral college	first ladies	term limits

Sharks

READ:

Relics of the past, sharks are the ultimate survivors. They constantly move about in the oceans and often only attack people if threatened. They eat everything from microscopic plankton to larger fish and even mammals. While most people think of all sharks as predators, some are actually harmless. Sharks can vary in size from the small pygmy shark, which only grow to about eight inches long, to the gigantic whale shark, which can measure up to 65 feet in length. They are a unique group of species among the diverse creatures of the sea.

RESEARCH:

1. Sharks are fish. Like all fish, sharks have gills through which they breathe. However, they lack gill covers. While other fish lay eggs to reproduce, sharks give birth to live young. What other ways are sharks different from other fish? Create a poster that identifies some of the unique characteristics of sharks.

2. There are many different species of shark. Identify at least ten different sharks and create a shark mobile with the illustrations of the different sharks.

3. Between the *Jaws* movies and the sensationalist news coverage of shark attacks, sharks have the reputation as vicious man-eaters. However, this is usually not the case. What do different sharks eat? Which ones are the least dangerous to people? Which ones are the most dangerous to people? What can you do to reduce your chances of being involved in a shark incident?

4. Like all fish, the shark has many uses to people. Imagine you run a shark farm. Design a brochure that advertises the uses for your sharks.

5. Sharks serve an important role in the food chain of the ocean. Why are sharks essential to the balance of life in the ocean? What can we do to protect sharks, which in turn protects the oceans? Write a letter to the editor describing the value of sharks and why they should be protected.

RELATE:

plankton	tiger shark	shark cages
Dr. Eugene Clark	ovoviviparous	electroreceptors

Sports

READ:

Do you like to play sports? Maybe you like to watch sports, or collect sports memorabilia. Sports are an important part of every culture in the world, although different groups prefer different sports. In the United States, baseball is often called our national pastime. Australians prefer rugby, and the British and Indians enjoy cricket. Soccer, or football as it is called in the rest of the world, is almost universally popular. Sports teach people about fair competition, team spirit, and good health.

RESEARCH:

1. Coaches must prepare players for lots of hard work, practices, winning, and losing. Make a list of qualities coaches must have. Which is the most important? List some great coaches who have had these qualities.
2. Select a sport popular in another country, such as cricket or jai alai. Who plays this game? How is it played? What kind of equipment is needed? Design a poster detailing all this information about your chosen sport.
3. What can you find out about the first Olympics? Why were they held? What were some of the events? Who were the competitors?
4. Many sports have a Hall of Fame. Choose one and write a travel brochure about it. Where is it located? Who is commemorated in it? Include this and any other information a tourist would want to know about visiting your chosen Hall of Fame.
5. What happened to baseball during World War II? Who took over playing baseball? Write a short story from the point of view of one of the new players.

RELATE:

Stanley Cup	stadiums	Wimbledon
Abner Doubleday	marathons	lacrosse

Television

READ:

First seen in America in 1927, television has had an important role in shaping American culture, both here and abroad. The first television sets were huge pieces of furniture with tiny screens. They were so expensive that, by 1945, only 5,000 homes owned one. Watching popular shows like "Texaco Star Theater" or "I Love Lucy" was a community event, because often, only one family in the neighborhood owned a television. Since that time, television has changed dramatically. From the original three broadcast stations, people can now choose from hundreds of cable and satellite stations. Streaming video can be watched on computers and even cell phones. Television will no doubt continue to evolve and shape our culture.

RESEARCH:

1. As long as there has been television, there have been commercials. Some commercials were so popular that their slogans were better known than the product. A classic from the 1980s was "Where's the beef?" from a commercial for Wendy's®. What are some other classic commercials that have become part of our cultural language? Create a list of memorable commercial slogans and the products they were marketing.

2. Television is regulated by the Federal Communication Commission. Create a brochure about the FCC. Where is it located? Who is in charge? How do they regulate television?

3. Everyone knows how to operate a television, but do you know how a television really works? Design a poster that illustrates how a television receives and displays picture and sound. Be sure to note the differences between vacuum-tube televisions and the newer plasma, LCD, and HD televisions.

4. The Emmys are awards given to the best television shows and performers every year. If you were in charge of the Emmys, who would you give awards to for best actor and actress, best comedy and drama, and others? Count all the votes in your class. Hold a ceremony where you hand out awards to the shows that got the most votes.

5. The average American watches 3.5 hours of television a day. How much television do you watch? Are you above average or below? What shows do you watch? Why?

RELATE:

coaxial cable	Nielsen ratings	satellites
networks	Milton Berle	Bill Cosby

© Mark Twain Media, Inc., Publishers

Time

READ:

The concept of time has occupied humans since the dawn of civilization. Today, we measure time in seconds, minutes, hours, days, months, and years, but it wasn't always like that. Early people used the sun and moon to keep track of hours and the seasons to keep track of years. As time passed, the methods and instruments designed to measure time became more sophisticated. The ancient Babylonians were the first to use the idea of 12 months. By the time of the Roman Empire, the Julian calendar was widely used, to be replaced later by the Gregorian calendar. To measure hours, first the sundial and, later, the hourglass were ways for people to keep track of time. In 1386, the first clock was constructed in England. It used a pendulum-like structure to measure time. By the sixteenth century, timepieces were common across Europe. Now we have clocks in our cars, homes, phones, computers, and other places. The better we are able to track time, the more important it has become.

RESEARCH:

1. We know that there are seven days in the week, but where did the idea of a week come from? How did the seven days get their names? Write a brief report that explains where the week came from and how the days got their names.

2. What are time zones? When were they established? Why are time zones important? If it is 3:00 P.M. in Huntsville, Alabama, what time is it in Boulder, Colorado? Paris, France? How many time zones are there in the United States? How many time zones are there in the world? Design a poster that provides information about time zones.

3. What is a leap year? How often do we have a leap year? Why do we need to have one? What makes people born on February 29th special? Write a short summary and present it to the class.

4. "Time is money" is a common saying. It means time is a commodity that is as valuable as gold or silver. What are some other common time sayings? What do they mean?

RELATE:

Mayan calendar	Archimedes clock	Stonehenge
Daylight Saving Time	Greenwich Mean Time	International Date Line

© Mark Twain Media, Inc., Publishers   53

Unusual Plants

READ:

Plants and shrubs are everywhere. Usually, when we think of plants, we think of the flowers, bushes, and trees planted around our homes and parks. We know that there are many plants, such as broccoli or strawberries, that are good to eat. We may even know that plants can be a source of medicinal remedies, like aspirin being derived from the bark of the willow tree. But the plant kingdom has a lot more variety than that. There are plants that tell time, predict the weather, eat meat, or even poison animals that try to eat them. Plants can be very strange.

RESEARCH:

1. The butterwort and pitcher plants have unusual features. What makes these plants special? Create a leaf-shaped booklet that illustrates these strange plants and explains what makes them unique.
2. There is a plant that is the largest living thing on Earth. What is it? How big can it get? How long does it live? How much bigger is it than the largest living animal? Design a poster that illustrates all these facts.
3. We get many medicines from plants. In addition to aspirin, what are some other medicines derived from plant sources? Create a brochure that lists medicines and the plants from which they come.
4. What are all the ways you use plants every day? Write a brief summary that lists all the ways plants play an important role in your life. Be sure to include any material made from a plant, such as cotton or paper. Share your list with the class.
5. One way plants are classified is by the type of seeds they produce. What are the different kinds of seeds? What plant produces the most seeds? The fewest? Which plant has the biggest seeds? The smallest? What kinds of seeds can you find around your home or school?

RELATE:

century plant   bonsai   hydroponics
topiary   Methuselah   kelp

© Mark Twain Media, Inc., Publishers   54

Volcanoes

READ:

Volcanoes are one of the most spectacular forces nature has to offer. Erupting molten rock, or magma, escapes when underground pressures grow too great. A vent is forced upward, and an eruption of magma occurs. More than 1,800 degrees, magma quickly cools on the surface and turns into lava. Pouring over the edge of a vent, lava can build layer upon layer to create volcanoes. Active volcanoes can be seen in Hawaii, Italy, Japan, and Africa. The eruptions these volcanos produce contain carbon dioxide, nitrogen, hydrochloric acid, and sulfur vapors. With the intense heat and poisonous gases, volcanoes can produce great devastation in very little time. When an eruption occurs, ash and debris can cover miles of ground in seconds. Volcanoes are a natural phenomenon that continue to inspire fear and respect in the people who live around them.

RESEARCH:

1. In May 1980, Mount St. Helens erupted in the United States. What happened to the volcanic cone of Mount St. Helens? What happened to the people who were nearby? Write a newspaper article about this event and what has happened since that eruption. Be sure to include a title.

2. Are volcanic eruptions predictable? How does a scientist predict an eruption? What kinds of equipment do they need? How accurate are the predictions? Design a poster that details the information you find.

3. Volcanic lava has built countless islands throughout the world. The Hawaiian islands were formed by volcanoes over many years. How long did it take for the islands to form? What did they look like 1,000 years ago? 10,000 or more years ago? Are they done growing? What will the islands look like in 10,000 years? 100,000 years? Construct a diagram that shows what the Hawaiian islands looked like and what you think they will look like in the future.

4. The eruption of Krakatoa in 1883 was perhaps one of the most violent volcanic events of all time. Where is Krakatoa? What happened to the area around it when it erupted? How did the eruption impact the weather that year? Describe this event in a short report.

RELATE:

Ring of Fire	Pompeii	Mt. Kilimanjaro
volcanology	Mt. Etna	Vulcan

Volunteering

READ:

In 1961, President John F. Kennedy challenged college students to serve their country by living and working in other countries. Since that time, over 180,000 volunteers have served in the Peace Corps by working in 138 countries. They assist with health care, environmental conservation, basic education, and technological development. The Peace Corps provides Americans with an opportunity to not only share their knowledge and expertise, but also their values. The Peace Corps is an on-going program open to all individuals who want to perform valuable services while also enriching their lives and the lives of others.

RESEARCH:

1. What are the requirements to enroll in the Peace Corps? Would you join the Peace Corps? Who are some famous people who have served in the Peace Corps? Create a brochure that answers these questions about the Peace Corps.

2. The International Red Cross is a large organization dedicated to improving the health of people in good times and in bad. Construct a time line of its development. When was it started? When did it become international? During what types of events has the Red Cross helped people? Contact your local Red Cross chapter for more information.

3. Are there service clubs in your school? Select one and interview the sponsor. What are their goals? Who benefits from the services? How are they supported financially? What does it take to join their club or organization?

4. Charitable organizations always need volunteers. What kinds of organizations need volunteers in your community? Make a list of all the organizations that need volunteers. What are the types of services volunteers can provide?

RELATE:

Clara Barton	Florence Nightingale	Hull House
Albert Schweitzer	philanthropy	Bill Gates Foundation

© Mark Twain Media, Inc., Publishers

Wind

READ:

> When the wind is in the east, it's good for neither man nor beast.
> — folk saying

What is wind? Wind is the movement of air over the surface of the earth. Wind can be gentle and warm, like a summer breeze, or ferocious and violent, like a tornado. Wind affects and is affected by climactic changes, clouds, storms, and even temperature. Measured in miles per hour or kilometers per hour, wind information is used to help meteorologists predict weather conditions and temperature. A strong, sudden gust of wind could tell of a coming storm, a soft breeze could ease the summer heat, or a biting wind could make a cold day feel much colder.

RESEARCH:

1. Wind can work for us by providing an inexpensive source of energy. Special windmills have been designed for capturing the wind's power. How does a windmill change wind into electricity? Construct a model of a windmill and label how it works.

2. What is the Beaufort Wind Scale? For what do meteorologists use it? Draw a poster that illustrates the wind scale and shows how it is used.

3. Wind words abound. Sometimes they relate to moving air, but other times, they are not associated with actual wind. Write a list of wind-related words and phrases. What do they mean? Which ones are weather-related, and which ones aren't? Make a list and share it with your class.

4. Tornadoes are a powerful force of nature. In the United States, tornadoes frequently occur in an area known as Tornado Alley. Where is Tornado Alley located? Approximately how many tornadoes occur there every year? Write a brief summary detailing information about Tornado Alley.

5. With the right weather conditions, tornadoes can occur almost anywhere. What should you do if a tornado is spotted near your house or school? How should you protect yourself? What should you do if you are in a vehicle? Prepare a brochure that informs readers what to do in the event of a tornado emergency.

RELATE:

cyclones	meteorology	water spouts
anemometer	*The Wizard of Oz*	Fujita Tornado Intensity Scale

Curriculum Areas by Topic Index

Science:

Animal Kingdom, Apples, Astronomy, Aviation, Bones, Botany, Caves, Chemistry, Color, Deserts, Dinosaurs, Disasters, Fossils, Insects, Oceanography, Optical Illusions, Sharks, Unusual Plants, Volcanoes, Wind

Math:

Architecture, Bridges, Geometry, Mathematics, Measurement, Money, Numbers, Time

Language Arts:

Authors, Biographies, Circus, Communication, Drama, Great People, Language Arts, Mythology, Newspapers, Paper, Poetry, Television

Social Studies:

Careers, Continents, Cowboys, Culture, Energy, Genealogy, Geography, Invention, Kites, Maps, Monuments, Music, Presidents

Life Science:

Food; Peanuts, Popcorn, Pizza!; Sports; Volunteering

© Mark Twain Media, Inc., Publishers

Standards by Topic Index

Each *Research* topic is matched with national standard skills. They contain other interrelated standards that will blend with those of your state.

1. **Animal Kingdom:** recognize interaction between humans and their environment
2. **Apples:** appreciate properties of physical texture
3. **Architecture:** identify a career area involving the analysis of two- and three-dimensional shapes
4. **Astronomy:** recognize the vastness of the universe and Earth's place in it
5. **Authors:** identify different authors' purposes or point of view
6. **Aviation:** understand that science and technology are interwoven
7. **Biography:** identify the defining characteristics of noted people
8. **Bones:** identify the structural basis of living things
9. **Botany:** recognize the variety of biodiversity
10. **Bridges:** understand figural properties applied in real-life proportions
11. **Careers:** identify organizations within society and their changes over time
12. **Caves:** know mechanical and chemical activities that shape and reshape the earth
13. **Chemistry:** understand that all matter has observable properties
14. **Circus:** use historical sources of information gathering
15. **Color:** describe properties of matter
16. **Communication:** identify the multiple media tools to enhance communication
17. **Continents:** recognize divisions on Earth's surface
18. **Cowboys:** understand how historical periods influence events
19. **Culture:** understand factors that influence the perception of places and regions
20. **Deserts:** recognize a process
21. **Dinosaurs:** understand organisms and their relationship to the whole
22. **Disasters:** recognize patterns within and across systems
23. **Drama:** understand the wide range and form of literature
24. **Energy:** identify forms of energy and consequences of using limited resources
25. **Food:** promote benefits of positive health practices
26. **Fossils:** understand organisms and their relationship to the whole
27. **Genealogy:** know relative value of a source of information
28. **Geography:** identify and compare geographic information
29. **Geometry:** explore concepts of geometric shape and contributions of great mathematicians

Standards by Topic Index (cont.)

30. **Great People:** synthesize and separate collected material
31. **Insects:** compare patterns within systems
32. **Invention:** understand the importance of technological development and its influences
33. **Kites:** identify a custom from a historical period and its development
34. **Language Arts:** synthesize and separate information from a variety of sources
35. **Maps:** use various map forms to process geographic information
36. **Mathematics:** understand different ways numbers are used
37. **Measurement:** use and measure quantities in the real world
38. **Money:** identify units involving measurements of money
39. **Monuments:** demonstrate knowledge regarding functions of a government agency
40. **Music:** know a social institution significant of Eastern and Western civilizations
41. **Mythology:** respond to a form of fiction by interpreting how the information is applied to life
42. **Newspapers:** analyze methods that effectively communicate ideas and information
43. **Numbers:** understand that numbers can be represented in a variety of forms
44. **Oceanography:** express interdependence of man and the environment
45. **Optical Illusions:** understand forces acting on an object
46. **Paper:** organize and interpret the order of written information
47. **Peanuts, Popcorn, Pizza!:** analyze validity of health information and services
48. **Poetry:** use a speaking strategy effectively
49. **Presidents:** understand the impact of significant people and their ideas
50. **Sharks:** identify the nature of living things
51. **Sports:** use effective skills that enhance health
52. **Television:** use responsive listening skills
53. **Time:** use concrete models and formulas for finding time
54. **Unusual Plants:** recognize diversity of living things
55. **Volcanoes:** identify a natural force and its effects on the environment
56. **Volunteering:** understand a role of the citizen in American democracy
57. **Wind:** recognize a force of energy

© Mark Twain Media, Inc., Publishers